D1795314

上海杂货铺 1930-1940年代 Shanghai housewares in the 1930s to the 1940s

nese Hardware Store.

设计师店"茶缸"内陈列的日用杂货，徐汇区，2005
Miscellaneous things displayed in the designer outlet "Cha Gang" (meaning "teacup") Xuhui District, 2005

中山西路上的竹器店，松江区，2009
Bamboo shop on Zhongshan Road W., Songjiang District, 2009

练塘镇一家制作杆秤的店铺，青浦区，2006
A steelyard-manufacturing shop in Liantang Town, Qingpu District, 2006

穿行于里弄民居卖晾衣竹竿的人，虹口区，2009
A peddler of laundry poles in a residential neighborhood, Hongkou District, 2009

设计师店"起想"对传统杂货的再设计，黄浦区，2004
The rediscovery of traditional designs in the designer outlet "Suzhou Cobblers", Huangpu District, 2009

上海老城厢内的沿街杂货店，黄浦区，2008
Roadside shops in the Shanghai Old Town, Huangpu District, 2008

弹棉花的人，长宁区，2012
A fluffing cotton filler, Changning District, 2012

六灶镇上的鞋铺，南汇区，2007
A shoemaker's shop on an old street of Liuzao Town, Nanhui, 2007

雁荡路（近淮海中路）上贩卖杂货的三轮车，黄浦区，2013
A peddling tricycle on Yandang Road, near Huaihai Road M., Huangpu District, 2013

策划：江岱，姜庆共

Curators: Jiang Dai, Jiang Qinggong

创作指导：陈丹燕

Creative Director: Chen Danyan

责任编辑：张翠

Editor: Zhang Cui

摄影、插图：周祺

Photographer, Illustrator: Zhou Qi

翻译：梁瀚杰

Translator: Liang Hanjie

封面插图、书籍设计：姜庆共

Cover Illustrator, Book Design: Jiang Qinggong

鸣谢：陈天星，陈志刚，高秀娟，顾慧珠，
顾金仙，顾月香，华雪娟，黄金善，
黄林芳，沈才英，盛雪娟，陶情健，
王宏春，魏鹏飞，杨忠奇，张凤仙，
赵仕德，朱金林，朱丽琴

Acknowledgements: Chen Tianxing,
Chen Zhigang, Gao Xiujuan, Gu Huizhu,
Gu Jinxian, Gu Yuexiang, Hua Xuejuan,
Huang Jinshan, Huang Linfang, Shen Caiying,
Sheng Xuejuan, Tao Qingjian, Wang Hongchun,
Wei Pengfei, Yang Zhongqi, Zhang Fengxian,
Zhao Shide, Zhu Jinlin, Zhu Liqin

曹可欣，Chen Chunqing，陈燕，韩峰，
胡惠萍，胡卫娣，Jack Newby，John Sunyer，
Kimi Tang，李钧鹏，林培君，林清，
刘大鸿，陆潇，陆忠华，罗英，屠爱军，
马德岗，马神龙，Rurd Absaroka，
Suger Tang，唐骋华，唐凌洁，汤惟杰，
吴南瑶，徐勤，周康华，中田美佐

Cao Kexin, Chen Chunqing, Chen Yan,
Han Feng, Hu Huiping, Hu Weidi, Jack Newby,
John Sunyer, Kimi Tang, Li Junpeng, Lin Peijun,
Lin Qing, Liu Dahong, Lu Xiao, Lu Zhonghua,
Luo Ying, Misa Nakata, Tu Aijun, Ma Degang,
Ma Shenlong, Rurd Absaroka, Suger Tang,
Tang Chenghua, Tang Lingjie, Tang Weijie,
Wu Nanyao, Xu Qin, Zhou Kanghua

同济大学出版社
Tongji University Press

SHANGHAI VIEW

Shanghai
Housewares

上海杂货铺

同济大学出版社
TONGJI UNIVERSITY PRESS

周祺著　Zhou Qi

州桥沿街的竹器摊　嘉定区　2006 Roadside bamboo shops in Zhouqiao, Jiading District, 2006

前言 Preface

　　杂货，在生活中随处可见：家务、炊煮、工作、娱乐……是我们了解不同地区生活方式和文化传统的途径之一。杂货大都出自不知名的工匠，其手工制作技艺，经家传或师徒传承，一部分由集群生产成为早期城市工业和经济发展的基础，一部分则仍然保持着个体手工制作、自由买卖的状态。

　　本书用摄影和插图的方式，呈现在上海仍然可以买到的120件杂货，并以竹、木、草、铁、布五种材质为线索，记录了10多位生活在上海的手工业者，通过他们的叙述及制作的产品，展现与分享手工业者的现状及本地的生活细节，为热爱生活的读者、中外设计师以及关注上海的人们带去自然和环保的生活信念。

The numerous items of everyday material culture that we employ in housework, cleaning, cooking, office work and entertainment are more than mere disposable objects; in a sense, they represent one of the ways for us to understand the idiosyncratic lifestyles and traditions of various places and peoples. A great number of these household items and daily necessities come from the handiwork of anonymous craftsmen, who have learned their skills through family inheritance or apprenticeship. While a majority of such craftsmen have been integrated into the urban workforce as a result of industrialization and economic development, a few have retained their old ways of artisanal working and continue selling their products themselves.

120 selected items of everyday use, currently available in Shanghai in one way or another, are shown in this book through photos and illustrations. The book also includes interviews with a dozen craftsmen living in Shanghai, who specialize in bamboo, wood, straw, iron and cloth, in order to portray and share the endeavors of the craftsmen as a whole as well as the intimate details of the lives in Shanghai. Hopefully, this book will help to introduce the ideas of environmental friendliness and resource preservation to readers with a love for life, to international designers looking for novel concepts, and to people who care about the development of Shanghai.

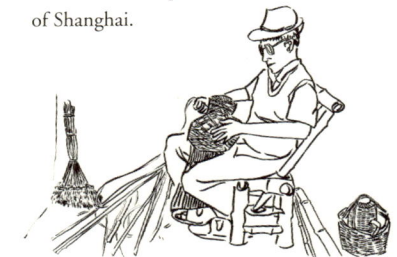

目录

这手工活用的都是巧劲

口述：陈师傅，白铁匠

我们老人家吧，还是喜欢土布的，耐用呀，穿着舒服呀　口述：张阿婆，织布手作人

¥29 竹蛇
¥30 春联
¥30 竹壳热水瓶
竹壳热水瓶制作过程
¥30 铅桶
¥30 菜篮

以前每家每户都不止有
一个篮子 口述：朱师
傅，竹编手作人

¥30 空竹
¥35 晾衣竹竿
¥35 草拖鞋
草拖鞋制作过程

草编在我们徐行都是祖
传的 口述：顾阿姨，
草编手作人

¥38 台罩
¥38 蒸笼
蒸笼制作过程

老早（以前）上海卖蒸
笼的有100多家 口述：
魏师傅，竹编手作人

¥38 布鞋
¥40 土布挎包
土布织布过程

织布是门技能，跟烧
饭、洗衣服什么一样
口述：沈阿姨，织布
手作人

土布花纹
¥45 烧水壶
¥45 元宝篮
元宝篮制作过程

我们做篮子要做的光
爽，除了实用，还要讲
卖相的 口述：赵师
傅，竹编手作人

¥45 算盘
¥45 浇水桶
浇水桶制作过程
¥45 套鞋
¥48 自行车儿童座椅
¥50 竹椅
¥50 锅铲
锅铲制作过程
¥59 竹席
¥60 竹窗帘
¥65 棉鞋
¥75 木砧板
¥80 兔子灯
兔子灯制作过程

现在就是没有接班人，
只要有人想做我就不做
了 口述：王师傅，兔
子灯手作人

¥86 躺椅
¥88 草席
¥90 草编包
¥100 筛
¥100 铜勺子
¥120 汤婆子
¥130 棉花胎
¥130 洗脚盆
洗脚盆制作过程

只有自己做的自己卖，
才能叫作坊 口述：
杨师傅，圆作手作人

¥255 藤椅
¥260 铁锅
铁锅制作过程

做这行需要技术，也需
要力气 口述：陶师
傅，熟铁匠

店铺、博物馆
推荐读物
创作过程

Contents

Clever skills are needed in this kind of manual work
Narrator: Mr. Chen, tinker

¥10 cotton gloves
¥10 porcelain cup
¥10 bamboo planer
¥12 bamboo whistle
¥12 strainer
¥15 chopsticks container
¥15 cattail-leaf fan
¥15 hula hoop
¥15 ashtray
¥15 wooden stool
¥15 rattle drum
¥15 washboard
¥15 apron and sleeves
Clothes made of homespun cloth

Old people like us prefer homespun cloth which is durable and comfortable *Narrator: Ms. Zhang, cotton cloth weaver*

¥16 water squirter
¥16 laundry pole
¥16 porcelain ornament
¥18 lace tablecloth
¥18 spittoon
¥18 feather duster
¥18 bouquet of artificial flowers
¥20 fish tank
¥20 hot water bag
¥20 mop
¥23 steelyard

¥25 rattan duster
¥25 cake mold
¥29 pillow
¥29 bamboo toy snake
¥30 Spring Festival couplets with the "auspicious" character in the center
¥30 thermos flask with bamboo casing
The manufacturing process of a thermos flask with bamboo casing
¥30 tin bucket
¥30 shopping basket

Each household used to own more than one basket *Narrator: Mr. Zhu, bamboo artisan*
¥30 diabolo
¥35 bamboo pole for drying laundry
¥35 straw slippers
The manufacturing process of straw slippers

Straw weaving is a family art in Xuhang *Narrator: Ms. Gu, straw weaver*

¥38 bamboo food cover
¥38 bamboo steamers

The manufacturing process of a steamer

There used to be over 100 makers of bamboo steamers in Shanghai *Narrator: Mr. Wei, bamboo artisan*

¥38 cloth shoes
¥40 homespun cloth bag
The weaving process of homespun cloth

Weaving cloth is a skill like any other, such as cooking and washing *Narrator: Ms. Shen, 58, cotton cloth weaver*

Patterns on homespun cloth
¥45 kettle
¥45 ingot basket
The manufacturing process of an ingot basket

We make premium baskets
that are not only useful
but also good-looking
*Narrator: Mr. Zhao, bamboo
artisan*

¥45 abacus
¥45 watering can
*The manufacturing process of
a watering can*
¥45 rubber shoes
¥48 bamboo children's
bicycle seat
¥50 bamboo chair
¥50 cooking spatula
*The manufacturing process of
a cooking slice*
¥59 bamboo mat
¥60 bamboo curtain

¥65 cotton-padded shoes
¥75 chopping board
¥80 rabbit lantern
*The manufacturing process of
a rabbit lantern*

I'll quit if I can find
someone as my worthy
successor   *Narrator: Mr.
Wang, rabbit lantern maker*

¥86 bamboo reclining chair
¥88 straw mat
¥90 straw-woven bag
¥100 sieve
¥100 brass spoon
¥120 bed warmer
¥130 cotton quilt padding
¥130 basin for washing feet

*The manufacturing process of
a foot-washing basin*

I sell what I make – that's
called a workshop
*Narrator: Mr. Yang, artisan
of circular objects*

¥255 rattan chair
¥260 iron wok
*The manufacturing process of
an iron wok*

This trade requires both
skills and strength
*Narrator: Mr. Tao, wrought
ironsmith*

¥15 蒲扇
palm-leaf fan

蒲葵叶 palm-leaf
33×30cm

价格；名称
price, name

材质，尺寸
material, size

¥: 人民币 (元) RMB (Yuan)
cm: 厘米 centimeter
Ø: 直径 diameter

请先阅读 Please read this first

　　本书中所涉及物品的价格、名称、造型、色彩、尺寸、材料，可能会因手工制作或购买地点不同而产生差异，以读者在购买地点所见实物为准。

　　本书中部分同季节或节庆有关的商品，并不是常年有售。部分产品可能不方便在某些交通工具上携带。

　　本书中的产品及相关信息采集时间：2006 - 2013年。

Each item shown in this book, produced by manual labor and purchased at a specific place and time, may differ from what you can find on the markets in terms of price, name, design, color, size and material. In case of discrepancies, what you actually get shall prevail.

Some items shown in this book are specific to certain seasons or festivals, and they may not be available all year round. Some items may not be allowed on certain public transport vehicles.

The items in this book as well as their relevant information are collected as of 2006 – 2013.

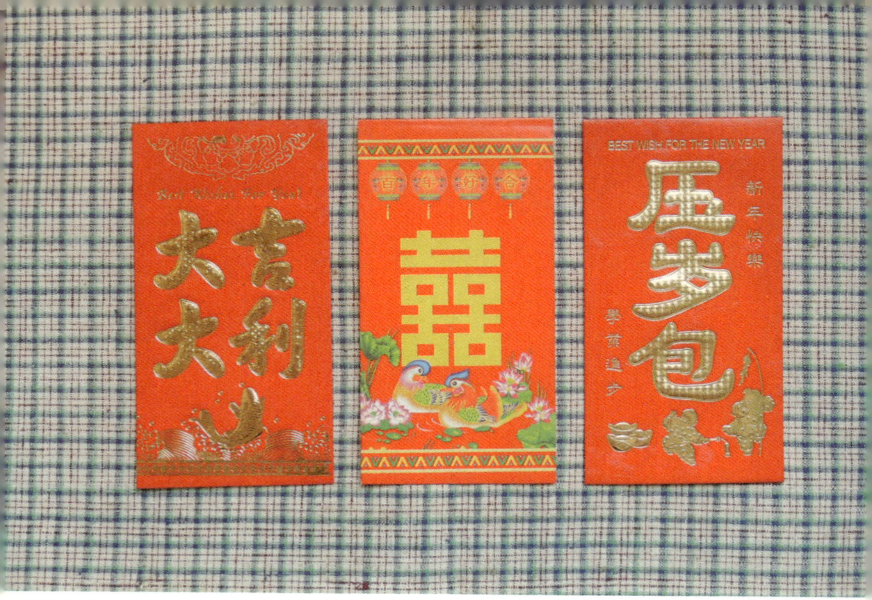

¥1 红包 (个)
red packet for gift money (each)

纸 paper, 17 × 9cm

In order to convey their good wishes, people give out gift money in these red packets, e.g. the New Year's money for children, the gift money for newlyweds, the bonus money for employees, etc.

¥1 竹尺
bamboo ruler

竹 bamboo, 3 × 10cm

Often used in cut-outs.

¥1 发夹 (组)
hairpins
(each set)

金属 metal
4.5cm

¥1 玻璃弹子 (个)
marble (each)

玻璃 glass, Ø1.5cm

¥1 掏耳勺
earpick

竹、棉
bamboo, cotton
16 × 2.5cm

¥1.5 毽子
shuttlecock

鸡毛、橡胶
chicken feather,
rubber
10 × 15cm

¥1.5 手帕
handkerchief

棉 cotton
28 × 28cm

¥2 铁皮青蛙
tin frog

金属 metal
4.5 × 7 × 5.5cm

¥2 板刷
scrubbing brush

竹、尼龙 bamboo, nylon
3.5 × 11.5 × 7cm

Often used for heavier clothes.
The Chinese characters made
of black nylon read "hygiene".

¥2 八脚架
clothes hanger
with 8 pins

竹、棉、金属
bamboo, cotton, metal
20 × 38cm

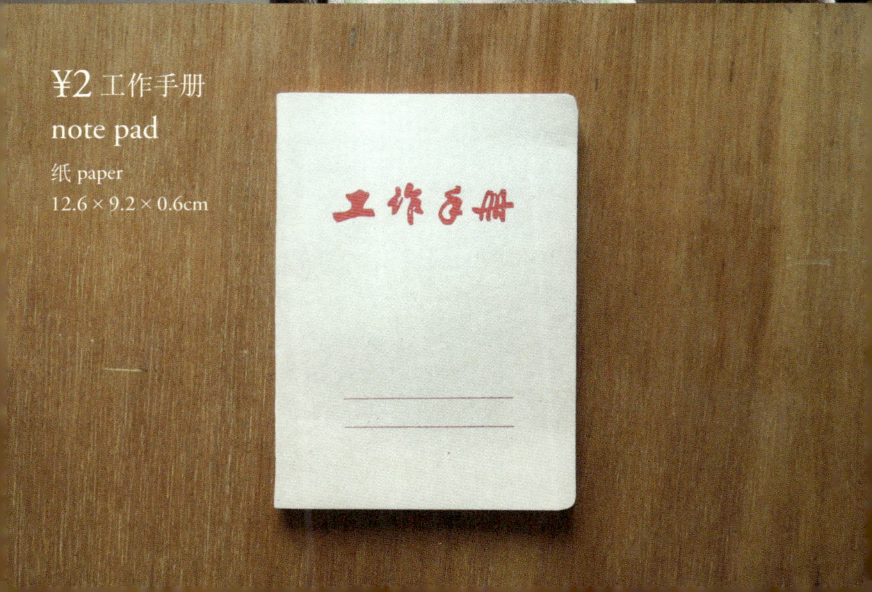

¥2 工作手册
note pad

纸 paper
12.6 × 9.2 × 0.6cm

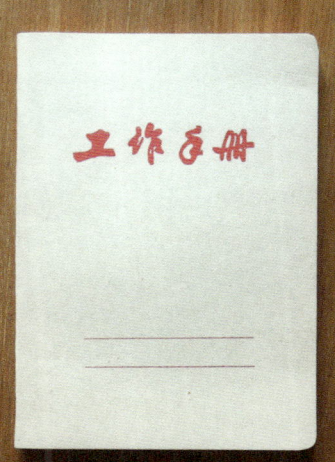

¥2 软尺
tape ruler

塑胶 plastic
Ø3cm, 160cm

¥3 苍蝇拍
fly-swatter

竹 bamboo
44 × 11cm

¥3 木夹子 (10个)
clothes pegs
(each set of 10)

木、金属
wood, metal
7 × 1.4 × 1cm

¥3 蛇皮袋
polypropylene
woven bag

塑料 Plastic

53 × 38 × 9cm

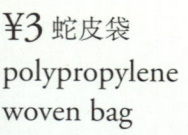

¥3 铁夹子
iron clip

金属 metal

8 × 9.3 × 3.6cm

¥3 竹蜻蜓
bamboo copter

竹 bamboo
17.5 × 15 × 2cm

¥3 锅垫
tablemat

竹 bamboo
Ø14,5cm

¥3 鞋刷
shoe brush

竹、尼龙
bamboo, nylon
2.5 × 21.5 × 3cm

¥3.8 玻璃杯
patterned glass cup

玻璃 glass
13 × Ø7.5cm

¥4 日历
calendar

纸、金属
paper, metal
16 × 11 × 1.9cm

¥4 塑料玩具
plastic toy
塑料 plastic
34 × Ø15cm

¥4 七巧板
tangram
木 wood
12 × 12 × 1cm

¥4 鞋垫
shoe-pad

棉 cotton
24 × 8cm

¥5 杯垫 (个)
tablemat (each)

黄草 Yellow straw
Ø9.5cm

¥5 烟花棒 (组)
sparklers (each set)

金属metal, 16cm

¥5 饭勺
rice ladle

竹 bamboo
20 × 6.5cm

¥5 草帽
straw hat

草 straw
10 × Ø42cm

¥5 剪刀
scissors

金属 metal
17.5 × 9cm

¥5 杯套 (个)
glass holder (each)

黄草 Yellow straw
7 × Ø7cm

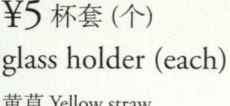

¥5 不求人
back-scratcher

竹 bamboo, 42 × 2.5cm

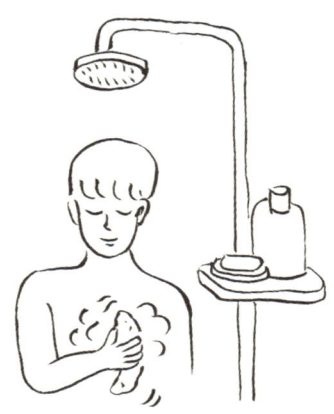

¥5 丝瓜筋
loofah

丝瓜 towel gourd
24 × 7cm

Made from a mature, dried
loofah gourd and used for
showering, back-scrubbing and
kitchen cleaning.

¥5 陀螺
whipping top
木 wood, 4.5 × Ø4.8cm

¥5 饭盒
lunchbox
铝 aluminum
6 × 21 × 12.5cm

¥5 卷发筒 (10个)
hair rollers
(each set of 10)

塑料 Plastic
7 × Ø3cm

¥5 蒲扇
cattail-leaf fan

蒲葵叶 palm-leaf
35 × 32cm

¥5 游戏棒
pick-up sticks

竹，木 bamboo, wood
18cm

¥5 丝刨
grater

木、金属
wood, metal
35 × 9cm

¥5 旅行剪刀
holding scissors

金属 metal
5.6 × 2.8cm

¥5 风车
pinwheel

竹、纸、金属
bamboo, paper, metal
33 × 11.5cm

¥5 信封 (10个)
envelope (each set of 10)

纸 paper
12 × 18cm

¥5 竹夹
bamboo tongs

竹 bamboo
23.5 × 17 × 2cm

¥6 信纸 (3本)
/letter paper
(each 3 pads)

纸 paper
26.7 × 19.3cm

¥6 擀面杖
rolling pin

木 wood
23 × Ø2.5cm

¥6 木梳
wooden comb
胶木 bakelite, 3×21cm

¥6 锅刷
pot brush
竹 bamboo
13.8×11×5.5cm

¥6.5 搪瓷杯
enamel mug

金属 metal
13 × 14cm

¥7 扫帚
broom

竹、芦花
bamboo, reed catkin
82 × 36cm

¥7 竹衣架
bamboo hanger

竹 bamboo
18.5×38cm

¥8 草编糖果盒
straw-woven
candy box

黄草 yellow straw
7.5×Ø11.5cm

¥8 蒸格
steaming lattice

竹 bamboo
3 × Ø16.5cm

¥8 浴罩
shower curtain

塑料 plastic, 200 × 100cm

In winter, a person taking
a bath in a home without a
proper bathroom must hang
a bath curtain on top of the
bathtub for the purpose of
keeping warm.

¥10 蛋饺勺
spoon for making egg
dumplings

金属、木 metal, wood
33.5 × Ø10.5cm

这手工活用的都是巧劲

口述：陈师傅，71岁，白铁匠，浦东新区新场镇

我17岁开始学敲铅皮（白铁），在厂里跟着老师傅学，平时下班的时候自己也练习练习。后来下岗了，就开始自己接活干了，到现在50多年了喔！

现在每天都要做8小时。做这个其实不是很用力的，敲敲打打都是用巧劲，所以也不算什么体力活，但刚学那会儿手一直敲出血，满手的橡皮膏。

一般经常做的尺寸我都已经在我脑子里了，其他有些比较复杂的，人家有要求的，我就画下来问他们是不是要这个东西。像浇花桶有6个尺寸，可以根据不同需要来定做。如头上的这个洞眼小一点少一点，水浇得就远一点，大一点密一点呢，就可以浇得近，每个定的人要求都不一样的。

我带过三个徒弟，不过现在都不做了，嫌这个赚钱慢。

店里做萝卜丝饼、油墩子用的那个勺卖得最好，5块钱一个，一天快的话可以做50个，看心情的。

逢年过节，像桃花节的时候人多得不得了，外国人也多，我已经做出名气来了，生意好得不得了，新场就我一家呀，每天有人跟我定东西，赚点功夫钱，吃喝没问题。

Clever skills are needed in this kind of manual work

Narrator: Mr. Chen, 71, tinker, Xinchang Town, Pudong

I began to work on tin at the age of 17 when I apprenticed myself to a veteran craftsman in the factory and practiced regularly after working hours. Later, after I was laid off from the factory, I began to take jobs on my own. That's already over 50 years ago today!

Now I work 8 hours every day. The work doesn't require much strength; instead, the tinkering needs a lot of clever skills. Therefore, it isn't really heavy manual labor. I kept injuring my fingers in the beginning though, and my hands were wrapped with tape all over to stop the bleeding.

Some common objects are so frequently produced that their sizes are already in my mind. As for more complicated objects to be custom-made for punters, I draw a design and ask them if this is what they want. For example, a watering can can be made in 6 sizes based on different needs, and it can produce a long spray of water if the holes at the top are made smaller and sparser, or produce a short spray of water if the holes are made larger and denser. I can custom-make all these items according to the needs of the customers.

I was the master of three apprentices, but they are all out of this business now, thinking it too slow in making money.

The best-selling item of my shop is the spoon for cooking carrot cakes and fried buns, at a price of RMB 5. I can make as many as 50 a day, but it depends on my mood.

During festivals, such as the Peach Blossom Festival, I have a great number of customers, even foreigners. I have established an excellent reputation, which brings me good business. My shop is one of a kind-in Xinchang, anyway! People place orders at my shop every day, and I can easily earn my meals with my skills.

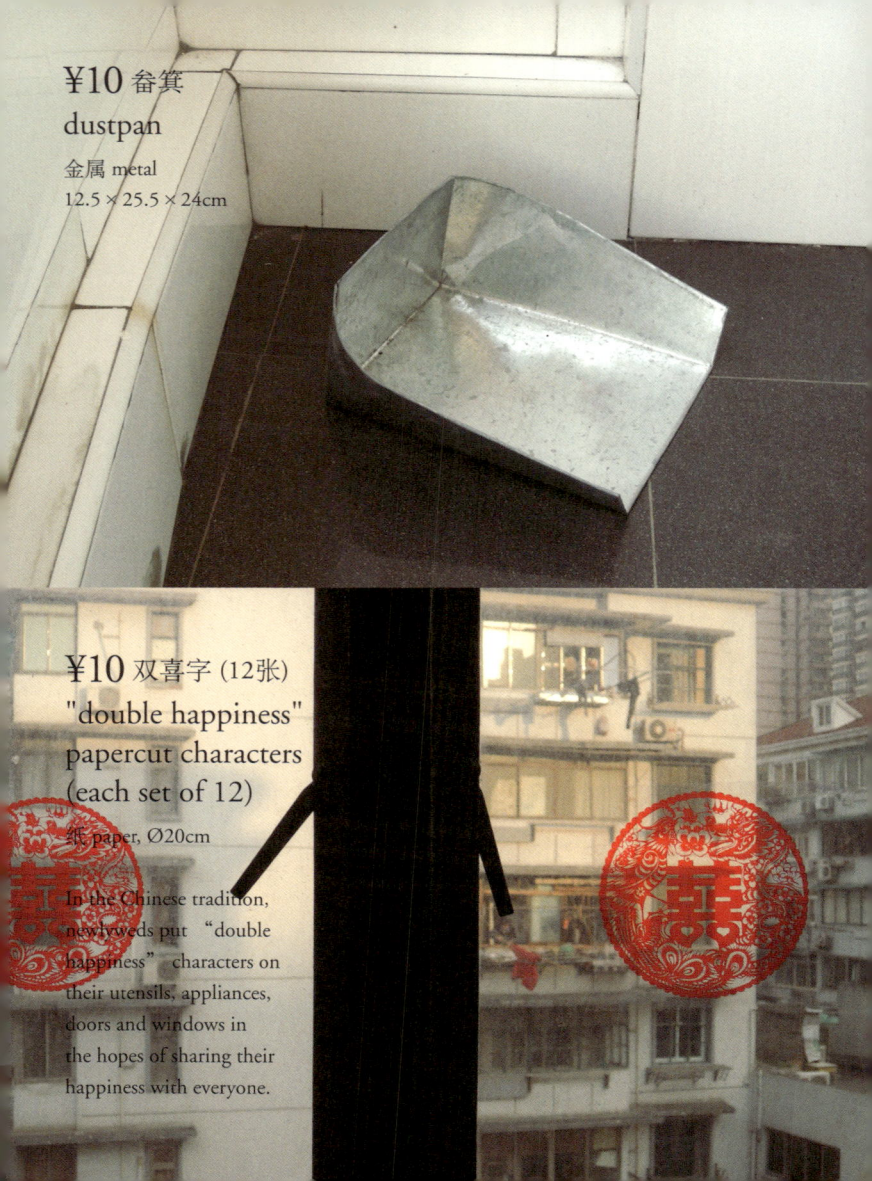

¥10 畚箕
dustpan

金属 metal
12.5 × 25.5 × 24cm

¥10 双喜字 (12张)
"double happiness"
papercut characters
(each set of 12)

纸 paper, Ø20cm

In the Chinese tradition,
newlyweds put "double
happiness" characters on
their utensils, appliances,
doors and windows in
the hopes of sharing their
happiness with everyone.

¥10 折扇
folding fan

竹、纸
bamboo, paper
33 × 60cm

¥10 淘米箩
bamboo basket for
washing rice

竹 bamboo
9 × Ø28cm

¥10 节约领
detachable collar

棉 cotton, 30 × 36cm

¥10 纱手套
cotton gloves

棉 cotton
21.5 × 15cm

¥10 陶瓷茶杯
porcelain cup

陶瓷 porcelain
14 × 12.5 × Ø8.5cm

¥10 竹刨

bamboo planer

竹、金属 bamboo, metal

14 × 5cm

¥12 哨子
bamboo whistle

竹 bamboo, 18 × Ø1.5cm

¥12 笊篱
strainer

竹 bamboo
49 × Ø18cm

¥15 筷筒
chopsticks container
竹 bamboo, 20 × Ø12cm

¥15 蒲扇
cattail-leaf fan
蒲葵叶 palm-leaf
36 × 27cm

¥15 呼拉圈
hula hoop

塑料 plastic, Ø62cm

¥15 烟灰缸
ashtray

玻璃 glass
3 × Ø11cm

¥15 木板凳
wooden stool

木 wood
21.5 × 22.5 × 12.8cm

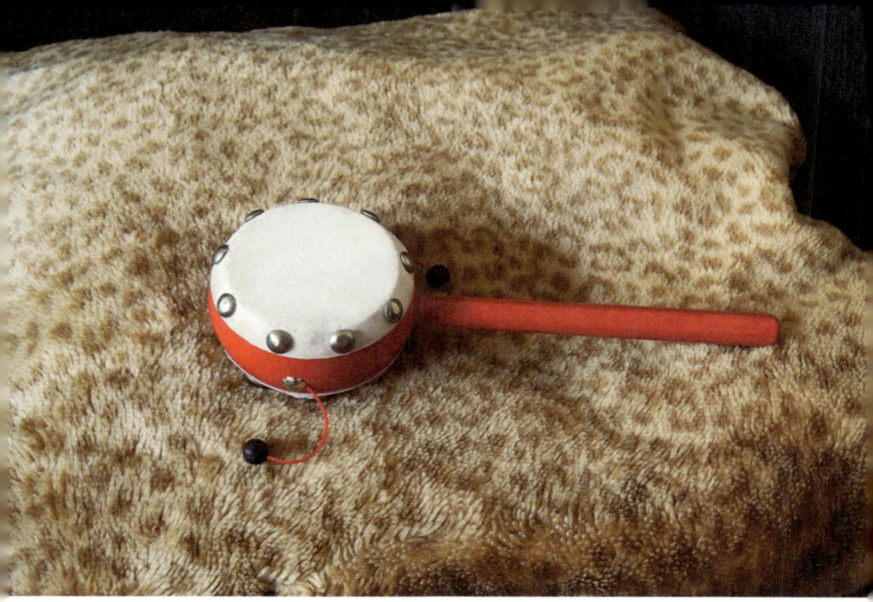

¥15 拨浪鼓
rattle drum

木、金属、猪皮
wood, metal, pig leather
20 × 4 × Ø7cm

¥15 洗衣板
washboard

木 wood
47.8 × 18 × 1.5cm

¥15 围裙，袖套 (组)
apron and sleeves
(each set)

棉 cotton
100 × 57cm
30 × 15cm

土布服装 Clothes made of homespun cloth

我们老人家吧，还是喜欢土布的，耐用呀，穿着舒服呀

口述：张阿婆，71岁，金山区亭林镇

　　我24岁嫁人后才开始跟婆婆学的织布，这里的小孩，一般都在10岁左右就开始学习织布和绣花了。我看我婆婆织了一天布，我就开始自己织了。我还教我女儿织过，她小学的时候，教她纺纱织布，不过到了她初中的时候，家里搬家，织布机就拆掉了，当柴烧掉了。

　　以前织布的原料，都是自己种棉花、采棉花，然后自己纺成一根根线，再去染坊染成自己要的颜色，颜料也都是纯天然的。一般织一块布可以做两件衣服，都自己做了自己穿。

　　提花布、条子布，通常用来做裤子；格子布，有大格子小格子，通常用来做包衫（外套）和衬衫；还有头巾布，因为夏天太阳很晒，冬天嘛又很冷，就遮块布在头上，做农活的时候还可以挡灰。土布吸水性好，透气性好，还可以做尿布，又是纯天然的棉，越洗越软，很好用的。还有全一色的布，用来做围裙的，除了这些，还可以做被套。零头布（边角料）可以做鞋子。

　　我们老人家吧，还是喜欢土布的，耐用呀，穿着舒服呀。

Old people like us prefer homespun cloth which is durable and comfortable

Narrator: Ms. Zhang, 71, cotton cloth weaver, Tinglin Town, Jinshan District

I got married at 24, at which point I learned to weave cotton cloth from my mother-in-law. The girls in this town usually learn weaving and embroidery at the age of 10. After seeing my mother-in-law weaving for a day, I started to weave on my own. I also taught my daughter to spin and weave when she was in elementary school. Unfortunately, when she was in junior high school, we moved to a new home and the weaving loom was taken apart and burned as firewood.

In the past, we wove cloth from home-grown and hand-picked cotton, which was spun into threads and dyed the desired colors in a dye-house. And the pigments for dyeing were made from natural materials, too! Usually a piece of homespun cloth can be used to make two pieces of clothing. We produce the homespun cloth, and we wear the clothes made from it.

Jacquard cloth and striped cloth can be used to make pants, while checkered cloth – both large checks and small checks – can be used to make jackets and shirts. We also make a kind of headscarf, which we wrap around our head to keep off sunlight in summer and cold winds in winter, as well as the dust from farm work. We make aprons with pure-color cloth. Of course, homespun cloth can be used to make bedsheets, and the offcut bits and pieces can be used for shoe-making. The homespun cloth has a lot of practical uses – even as diapers – because it boasts good water absorption, good ventilation, and great comfortableness because natural cotton gets even softer with each wash.

Old people like us prefer homespun cloth which is durable and comfortable.

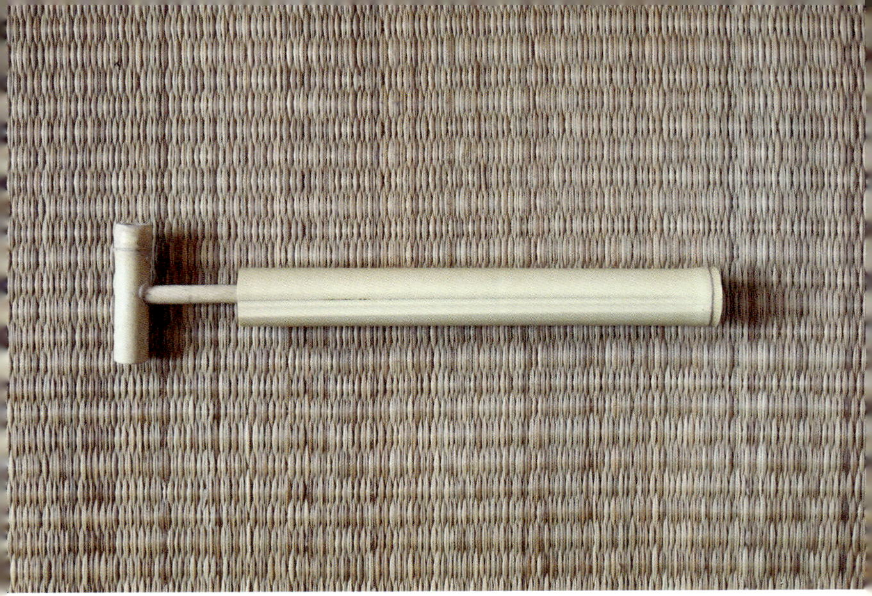

¥16 水枪

water squirter

竹、棉 bamboo, cotton
4 × 23 × Ø2.6cm

¥16 丫叉头

laundry pole

塑料 plastic
126 × 6cm

¥16 陶瓷摆设
porcelain ornament

陶瓷 porcelain
16 × 15 × 3.8cm

¥18 抽纱台布
lace tablecloth

棉 cotton, 120 × 120cm

¥18 痰盂罐
spittoon

金属、塑料
metal, plastic
25 × Ø21cm

¥18 鸡毛掸子
feather duster

鸡毛、竹
Chicken feather,
bamboo
75 × 15cm

¥18 人造花
bouquet of
artificial flowers

塑料、绢
plastic, thin silk
28 × 40 × 38cm

¥20 金鱼缸
fish tank

玻璃 glass
□ × Ø22cm

¥20 热水袋
hot water bag

橡胶、塑料 rubber, plastic
34 × 17.5cm

¥20 拖把
mop

塑料、棉
plastic, cotton
150 × 15cm

￥23 杆秤
steelyard

木、金属 wood, metal
46 × Ø25cm

¥25 藤拍
rattan duster

藤 rattan
70 × 28.5cm

¥25 糕模
cake mold
木 wood, 3 × 19 × 7.5cm

¥29 枕头
pillow
藤 rattan
8.5 × 37 × 15cm

¥29 竹蛇
bamboo toy snake

竹、金属 bamboo, metal
44 × Ø3cm

¥30 春联 (组)
Spring Festival
couplets with the
"auspicious"
character in the
center (each set)

纸 paper, 40 × 15cm
32 × 32cm

大吉大利

福

慶佳節順意平安

迎新春快樂祥和

¥30 竹壳热水瓶
thermos flask with
bamboo casing

竹、木、玻璃
bamboo, wood, glass
40 × Ø10cm

竹壳热水瓶制作过程 The manufacturing process of a thermos flask with bamboo casing

¥30 铅桶
tin bucket
金属，木 metal, wood
52 × 033 cm

¥30 菜篮
shopping basket
竹 bamboo, 45 × 30cm

以前每家每户都不止有一个篮子

口述：朱师傅，65岁，竹编手作人，青浦区朱家角镇

我学编篮子的时候，就在师傅边上看看，和师傅一起编，学了三个下午，就算是出师了，一开始都做不好的，慢慢的再自己摸索。

到了卖篮子的时候，大家摊子都搬在一起，然后就可以互相看到各自做的篮子，再从别人那里讨教些不同的编法，大家编的东西都一样，只是编法有所不同。

以前买篮子的大都是本地人，家家户户都要用的嘛，每户还不止有一个篮子，都是我当天做，当天就全部卖光了，能维持基本生活。现在买的人少了，所以还要靠养老金。

过去我们当地一些人家结婚还有个传统，就是要在篮子里装香烟、一条鱼、一只鸡，放满两个篮子，外面包一层红纸，这样就可以去娶亲了。还有装饭的篮子现在都还有人在用，就是把烧熟的米饭，直接放在篮子里面保存，盖子一盖就好了，这种天气（11月）不放冰箱也不会坏。

现在游客买的多，他们觉得稀奇，买一个回去挂家里装饰下也蛮好看的，怀旧一下。

Each household used to own more than one basket

Narrator: Mr. Zhu, 65, bamboo artisan, Zhujiajiao Town, Qingpu District

When I began to learn the weaving of bamboo baskets, I observed my master's work and practiced by assisting him. After studying like this for three afternoons, I was officially proclaimed a bamboo artisan. My work left much to be desired in the beginning, and I had to learn from trial and error.

On the market, all the basket booths were located in one place, so all the basket-makers could see each other's work. Naturally, a basket-maker would ask another about the methods of basket weaving. Basically they all worked in one general category – baskets, but the weaving methods were widely different.

In the past, my patrons were mostly local residents. Baskets were needed everywhere, and each household used to own more than one basket. Therefore, all the baskets I made for a day were often sold-out before nightfall, and the business was good enough for me to lead a satisfactory life. Now, the business is poor and I have to rely on my pension.

There used to be a nuptial tradition in my hometown: The bridegroom went to welcome the bride with two baskets filled with cigarettes, a fish and a chicken, covered with red paper. Even today, baskets are used as lunchboxes: Just put cooked rice and dishes in a basket and close the lid, as the food won't go bad in weather like this (in November).

Now my patrons are mostly tourists who are curious about baskets and are eager to have one as home decoration – for old time's sake, perhaps.

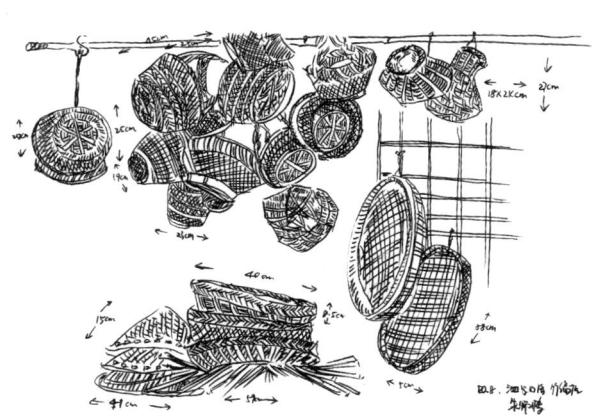

¥30 空竹
diabolo

竹、棉 bamboo, cotton
14.5 × Ø10cm
38.5 × 157cm

¥35 晾衣竹竿(根)
bamboo pole for
drying laundry

竹 bamboo, 250cm

¥35 草拖鞋
straw slippers

黄草 Yellow straw
21 × 8 × 3.8cm

草拖鞋制作过程 The manufacturing process of straw slippers

高阿姨 Ms Gao   顾阿姨 Ms Gu   顾阿姨 Ms Gu

草编在我们徐行都是祖传的

口述：顾阿姨（上中），60岁，草编手作人，嘉定区徐行镇

　　草编在徐行都是祖传的，家家户户都会做。我7岁时跟妈妈和奶奶学的，要学二三年，长大了，懂一点了，就越做越好了。刚开始的时候，大人不让我们做鞋面，只能编编鞋底，因为鞋面要做得漂亮，不然卖不掉。

　　编一双拖鞋至少要一天，如果在上面搞点花什么的，做得更精细点，要花两天功夫。鞋子不是人人会做的，有的人只会做草包，做草包方便，只要一个

手编就可以了。鞋子需要两个手一起做的，左右手都要会编。

　　每根草编出来什么样子我脑子里都想好的，一般都是我觉得一个颜色编得差不多了，就换个颜色来做花色。

　　黄草都是在本地种植的，刚收下来的时候是青的，要晒得干透干透，再封起来，放个半年才可以用，各种颜色有工厂专门来染，要什么颜色就染什么颜色。

　　我们一年四季都在编，平时边工作边聊聊天，就是编的时候头一直低着，颈椎一天下来有点吃不消。

　　现在当地小学里会有草编课，我们教会他们老师，让老师再去教小朋友，一个礼拜一次。

Straw weaving is a family art in Xuhang

Narrator: Ms. Gu (the person in the center in the previous photo), 60, straw weaver, Xuhang Town, Jiading District

Straw weaving is a family art in Xuhang. Every household is capable of it. I learned it from my mother and grandmother when I was 7, and I spent two to three years learning. After I grew up, I acquired some artistic understanding, and my work became better and better. At first I was not allowed to make insteps and had to content myself with making soles, because shoes are only marketable when they are good-looking on the insteps.

It takes at least a day to make a pair of straw slippers. If the slippers have a fancier design, like having a lot of ornaments, it will take longer, say two days, to finish a pair. Shoe-making is not for everyone, though; some people are only capable of making straw bags, because bags are easily done with one hand, while shoes are more difficult and must be worked on ambidextrously.

In my mind, there is a clear-cut plan of how each straw will turn out in the finished product. Usually when I feel I'm done with one color, I'll switch to another color for some variety.

All the yellow straws are grown locally. They are green when freshly harvested, and can't be used for weaving until they have been stashed indoors for at least six months after being completely sun-dried. They are dyed into whichever colors you can name at special dye-houses.

My fellow weavers and I work all year round, and we engage in happy chatter at work. My neck suffers a lot after a day's work, because I always have to bend my head down when weaving.

Now the local elementary school offers straw weaving lessons. We teach the teachers how to do straw weaving, and the teachers give the children a straw weaving lesson once a week.

¥38 台罩
bamboo food cover
竹 bamboo, 25 × Ø54cm

Often used in summer
to prevent food from
being polluted.

¥38 蒸笼 (组)
bamboo
steamers
(each set)
竹 bamboo
14 × Ø18cm

蒸笼制作过程 The manufacturing process of a steamer

解阿婆
Ms Xie

魏师傅
Master Wei

老早（以前）上海卖蒸笼的有100多家

口述：魏师傅，92岁，竹编手作人，虹口区海伦路

我爷爷老早在丹阳（江苏省）就开了家"顺昌蒸笼店"。我爸爸跟我爷爷学的，我是15岁的时候爸爸教我的，现在家里没人做蒸笼了，我是末代了。

1921年爸爸来上海开店，店开在楼下，人么住在楼上，爸爸过世后，店就交给我了。后来公私合营店关了，我就去一家工厂当会计，一直到70岁退休后，才重新开始再做的。现在每天要做2个小时的活，只要对身体没妨碍，我肯定会一直做下去。

老早是这样的，吃好早饭就开始干活，先把竹子锯开，然后预备今天要做多少个（蒸笼）就把料劈好，上午一定要全部劈好削好，下午开始做，到晚上竹子就变成蒸笼了。每天小的能做十几个，大的可以做五六个。

学徒的话，老早规矩学三年，还要再帮师傅做三年，头三年没有工资的，只有一些零用钱。

老早上海卖蒸笼的有100多家，蒸笼也有几十种花样。现在来买的居民比较多，还有些小饭店，也有人买来当道具拍电影的。

There used to be over 100 makers of bamboo steamers in Shanghai

Narrator: Mr. Wei, 92, bamboo artisan, Hailun Road, Hongkou District

My grandfather owned a bamboo steamer shop in Danyang, Jiangsu Province. My father learned to make bamboo steamers from my grandfather, and he taught me the skill when I was 15. Now, no one except me in my family makes bamboo steamers; I am the last generation of bamboo steamer makers.

My father came to Shanghai in 1921 to open a shop of bamboo steamers, and his family lived upstairs. When he passed away, the shop was handed down to me, though it was eventually shut down during the Socialist Reconstruction. I worked as an accountant in a factory until retiring at the age of 70. It is after my retirement that I picked up my former trade of making bamboo steamers. Now I work two hours a day on bamboo steamers, and I'll keep on doing this as long as my health permits.

The traditional rules of making bamboo steamers are like this: start working after breakfast; prepare the material by sawing bamboo into sections and slicing them into appropriate sizes according to the amount of steamers to make for that day; finish all the sawing and slicing by noon, and begin making steamers in the afternoon; make sure that all the prepared bamboo slices have been made into steamers by nightfall; in this way, the expected yield of a day will be a dozen small steamers or 5-6 big ones.

As for apprenticeship, the traditional rules are that the apprentice is to serve three years on probation and another three years as an assistant for the master; the apprentice is unpaid in the first three years and has to make do with a small allowance.

There used to be over 100 makers of bamboo steamers providing over 100 kinds of products in Shanghai. Now, my patrons are mainly individuals and eatery owners; in some rare cases, my steamers are used as movie props.

¥38 布鞋
cloth shoes
棉 cotton, 7 × 29 × 11cm

¥40 土布挎包
homespun cloth bag
棉 cotton, 25 × 30 × 8cm

土布织布过程 The weaving process of homespun cloth

织布是门技能，跟烧饭、洗衣服什么一样

口述：沈阿姨，58岁，织布手作人，奉贤区平安镇

我12岁开始学织布的。小时候，先是帮忙摇线，然后么织单色的、黑白条纹的花样，大点了就织方格子的花样。织布都要记花样的，要记性的。还要看个人本身聪明不聪明，有的小妹妹刚学就会了，有的到长大了都还不会。

织布就在家里的客厅里面，织布机都是借来借去的，谁家要用了么就拿去。织布机是有专门木匠做的，有些东西可以拆下来，搬运方便。

准备工作（穿纱）要一天时间，三四个人一起做呢。织布最难的地方就是花色（花样）多的时候，容易忘记踩踏板和穿梭的步骤。简单的花样两个踏板就可以解决了，复杂点的就要四个了，最多有五个踏板。一天么好织13尺，织好的布要洗一洗，晒晒干，再放在箱子里。

以前上班的，现在退休了，才开始又织布的。现在么地也还在，也种种菜。以前织布的人很多，因为自己要用呀，织不来的人少数的。现在这边的人，60岁左右的基本都会，是门技能嘛，跟烧饭、洗衣服什么一样。

Weaving cloth is a skill like any other, such as cooking and washing

Narrator: Ms. Shen, 58, cotton cloth weaver, Ping'an Town, Fengxian District

I learned to weave cotton cloth when I was 12. In the beginning I was too young to do anything, so I helped the adults spin cotton threads. Later, I worked on single colors or black-and-white stripes, then on checkered patterns when I grew older. Weaving requires a good memory, because all the patterns must be memorized. Therefore, a person with a clever mind will do well in weaving. Some girls learn it quickly at a young age, while some don't master the skill well into their adulthood.

Each household does weaving in the living room. The weaving loom is used on loan among several households, and whoever has weaving work to do may take it. The loom, built as a special carpentry job, has some removable parts for convenient transportation.

The preparation for weaving work, threading, takes 3-4 people a whole day to accomplish. The trickiest part of weaving is to do with the complexity of the patterns, as the weaver tends to blunder over the pedaling and shuttling procedures. A simple pattern requires only two pedals, a moderate pattern four, and the most complex pattern must be handled with up to five pedals. For a single day, I can produce 13 chi (4.3 meters) of cotton cloth, the finished cloth must be washed, sun-dried, and then kept in chests.

I had a job, but now I'm retired. That's why I do weaving. I still have my farmland, on which I grow some vegetables. In the past, a lot of people did weaving, because they needed the homespun cloth; few people were exempt from weaving work. Now, in this neighborhood, most people in their sixties can weave cotton cloth. Weaving is a skill like any other, such as cooking and washing.

土布花卷 Patterns on homespun cloth

¥45 烧水壶
kettle

金属 metal
17 × 30 × Ø22cm

¥45 元宝篮
ingot basket

竹 bamboo
28 × 43 × 33cm

These ingot-
shaped baskets,
formerly used in
food shopping, are
now used in grape
picking.

元宝篮制作过程 The manufacturing process of an ingot basket

我们做篮子要做的光爽，除了实用，还要讲卖相的

口述：赵师傅，78岁，竹编手作人，嘉定区徐行镇

我学生意的店叫"朱顺泰竹器行"，老师傅做，只给你看，编竹篱笆、蒸馒头的笼格、煤笋、夏天的凉席。我14岁前还在徐行读书，当时没办法呀，读书读不起呀，想着手艺人总归有饭吃的，所以就去学了。解放后，我在工地、建筑工程队搭毛竹架子，退休以后就在家里做篮子。

平时就6点去菜场，早出去风凉点，带三四只篮子出去卖，然后到8、9点钟回来。来买的基本上都是本地人，还有人批发去摘葡萄用。现在小篮子要的人多，但我不划算的呀，材料用的差不多，编大的可以卖贵一点。

篮子小嘛，蔑劈好，2个钟头可以编好了，快来西的，每天可以做三四个，有时还去茶馆喝点茶，然后回来再做会儿。做到六点，吃晚饭了。

最麻烦的是劈蔑。竹蔑买不到的，都是自己劈，然后要一根根刮，这样蔑就不毛了。我们做篮子要做的光爽，除了实用，还要讲卖相的，拿出去要像样的呀，考究的不得了。现在刮蔑的刀也买不到了，叫人家做也做不出来，因为他们都没见过呀。

We make premium baskets that are not only useful but also good-looking

Narrator: Mr. Zhao, 78, bamboo artisan, Xuhang Town, Jiading District

I took up apprenticeship at Zhu Shuntai's Bamboo Shop, where I observed the master's work and practiced on bamboo fences, steamers for buns, coal baskets, and mats. I quit school at the age of 14 – what could I do? I had to earn a living back then, and believed that the business of a craftsman could always provide me with bread. After 1949, I helped to build bamboo scaffolds on construction sites and projects. Since my retirement, I have been making bamboo baskets at home.

At 6 o'clock every day I go to the food market in the coolness of the morning, bringing with me three to four baskets for sale. Then I come back at 8 or 9 o'clock. The buyers are mostly local residents, and some people buy my baskets in bulk for grape-picking. A lot of people want small baskets now, but small baskets mean little profit for me. A basket, big or small, costs roughly the same amount of materials. If I produce a big basket, I can sell it for a higher price.

In the case of small baskets, I can make one in two hours after the bamboo slices are prepared – quite a quick proposition, isn't it? I can make three to four a day. Sometimes I visit a teahouse for a while, before coming back to my work. At 6 o'clock, it's time for dinner.

The trickiest part is of course preparing the bamboo slices, which are not buyable. I have to cut bamboos into slices and polish them individually to remove roughness. We bamboo artisans make premium baskets that are not only useful but also good-looking. The baskets must be presentable, right? One can't be too fastidious about that. What vexes me is that the polishing knives are no longer available now, and no one seems capable of making one because no one has seen such a knife.

¥45 算盘
abacus
木、金属 wood, metal
16 × 35 × 3cm

¥45 浇水桶
watering can
金属 metal
17 × 37 × Ø13cm

浇水桶制作过程·The manufacturing process of a watering can

¥45 套鞋
rubber shoes

橡胶 rubber
8 × 26 × 9cm

¥48 自行车儿童座椅
bamboo children's
bicycle

竹
60 × cm

¥50 竹椅
bamboo chair

竹 bamboo
70 × 39 × 30cm

¥50 锅铲
cooking spatula

金属 metal
30.5 × 9.8cm

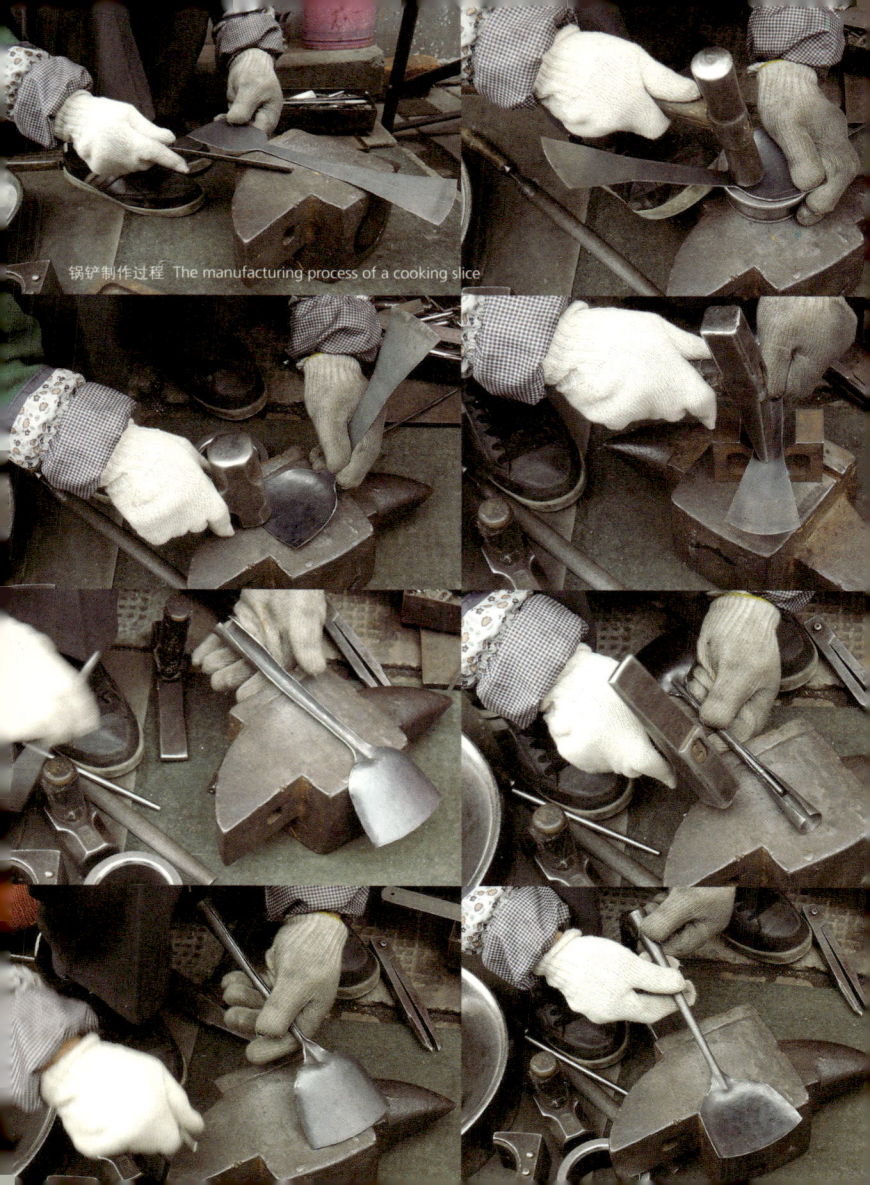

锅铲制作过程 The manufacturing process of a cooking slice

¥59 竹席
bamboo mat
竹、棉 bamboo, cotton
150 × 200cm

¥60 竹窗帘
bamboo curtain
竹、棉、木
bamboo, cotton, wood
100 × 150cm

¥65 棉鞋
cotton-padded shoes
棉 cotton
11 × 24.5 × 9.5cm

¥75 木砧板
chopping board
木 wood
21 × 33 × 2cm

¥80 兔子灯
rabbit lantern

纸、棉、竹、金属
paper, cotton, bamboo, metal
22 × 48 × 43cm

With a lit candle in it as
illumination, the lantern
is pulled along the streets
as a traditional toy for the
Lantern Festival (the 15th
day of the 1st month in the
Chinese lunar calendar).

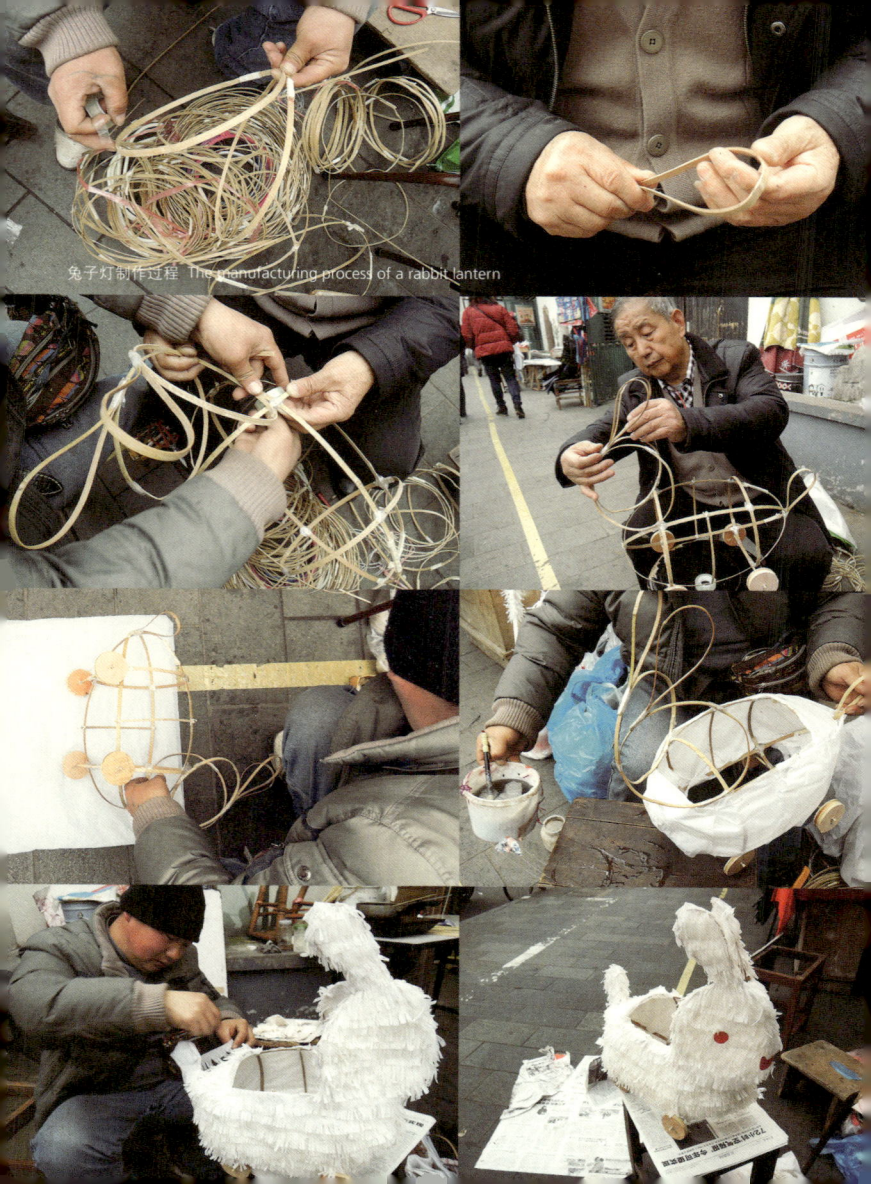

兔子灯制作过程 The manufacturing process of a rabbit lantern

王师傅
Master Wang

陈师傅
Master Chen

现在就是没有接班人，只要有人想做我就不做了

口述：王师傅，72岁，兔子灯手作人，浦东新区浦三路

　　我嬢嬢1950年代的时候编热水瓶壳子，她把单位里的竹蔑拿回来做兔子灯，我们从小就看到的呀，也没有特别教，看看就会了。那时候城隍庙也有卖兔子灯，也是像现在这样摆摊卖的，就过年的时候，正月半。

　　现在上海滩手工做兔子灯很少了。5年前，我利用过去做包装借的厂房想着是不是能恢复兔子灯的生产，

当时我们有4个人一起做，房租、工资、成本上去了，搞一年亏一年。今年开始我在家里做，就是每天要等女儿上班去之后才能开始。不过马上就要搬到新的工作室去了，那边地方宽敞，想做早点晚点都可以。

　　兔子灯最复杂的工艺是骨架的尺寸，要对称。骨架最早是用竹蔑做的，现在我尝试用包装带来做，也就是竹子弄不到了之后的一个替代品。算下来一年我也要做1500只兔子灯了，都是每天做做积累到过年的时候再卖。卖的最快的就是正月半那几天，本来城隍庙就有个灯会嘛。

　　现在就是没有接班人，只要有人想做我就不做了。

I'll quit if I can find someone as my worthy successor

Narrator: Mr. Wang, 72, rabbit lantern maker, Pusan Road, Pudong

In the 1950s, my aunt brought home some bamboo slices which were the leftovers of the casing of thermos flasks, and she made rabbit lanterns with those slices. It seemed that I learned to make rabbit lanterns by simply looking at them, without anyone teaching me! At that time, rabbit lanterns were sold in the Town God's Temple – on stalls, like today – around the Chinese New Year, especially on the Lantern Festival (the 15th day of the 1st month in the Chinese lunar calendar).

Today, it is hard to find handmade rabbit lanterns in Shanghai. Five years ago, I tried to find a way to restart the production of rabbit lanterns by making use of some factory space that I had rented for a packaging business. I had a team of five people to produce rabbit lanterns at the time, but as the costs – rent, wages, etc. – went up year by year, we registered increasing losses. From this year, I've been producing rabbit lanterns at home,

though I have to start after my daughter has left for work. Fortunately I will soon move to a new spacious studio, where I won't bother others with my wayward work schedules.

The most complex technique in making a rabbit lantern is to create a symmetrical skeleton. The skeleton is supposed to be made of bamboo slices, but now I try to make it with packaging bands because bamboo slices are hard to find. Every year I produce 1,500 rabbit lanterns in total, which I make on ordinary days and bring to the markets for the Chinese New Year. The first half of the 1st month in the Chinese lunar calendar is the best-selling window for my rabbit lanterns – they just go like crazy. There's this Lantern Party in the Town God's Temple, you know.

I'll quit if I can find someone as my worthy successor, but to my regret, I can't find anyone.

¥86 躺椅
bamboo
reclining chair

木、竹、金属
wood, bamboo, metal
57 × 85 × 12cm
57 × 85 × 86-110cm

¥88 草席
straw mat

草 straw
150 × 200cm

¥90 草编包
straw-woven bag

黄草 Yellow straw
53.5 × 37 × 13cm

¥100 筛
sieve

竹 bamboo
7 × Ø60cm

¥100 铜勺子
brass spoon

金属 metal
19 × 2.3cm

¥120 汤婆子
bed warmer

金属 metal
10 × Ø18cm

¥130 棉花胎
cotton quilt padding

棉 cotton,
180 × 210cm

This is the inside of a quilt, which often comprises two layers and can be put under the sheets for more warmth in winter.

¥130 洗脚盆
basin for washing feet

木、金属 wood, metal
17 × Ø36cm

洗脚盆制作过程 The manufacturing process of a foot-washing basin

只有自己做的自己卖，才能叫作坊

口述：杨师傅，70岁，圆作手作人，闵行区七宝镇

我们这个叫圆作，专门做圆的东西。还有种叫方作，是做椅子、家具的。我16岁跟师傅学手艺，到现在也有五十几年了，那个年纪开始学么，至少要学6年。

要质量好，一天做一个不错了。按照老法来做，木条要用竹钉穿起来的。不过，现在大多数时候都是用胶水粘起来，方便呀。我一般都用杉木，质地比较软，其他木料太硬了没办法手工弄的。一般都会挑树结少的木料，这样做出来好看，也不容易漏水。买来的木料要晒将近一个多月，要是做到一半天气不好受潮了，还要等天气好的时候再拿出来晒晒透。我这个是作坊，只有自己做的自己卖，才能叫作坊。

以前很多东西都要用到木桶，装饭的要饭桶，锅子么要锅盖，都用木头做的。现在冬天买脚盆的人比较多，天冷大家喜欢买高一点的，天热么都喜欢矮的，平时用来洗洗脚。新的木盆拿回去放点冷水给它泡着，吸收了水分以后呢，木头会胀开，这样它密度就高了，一点水都不会漏。

I sell what I make – that's called a workshop

Narrator: Mr. Yang, 70, artisan of circular objects, Qibao Town, Minhang District

Called an artisan of circular objects, I make basins and buckets. Of course, there are artisans of square objects, who make square things like chairs, tables and cupboards. I became an apprentice at the age of 16 – over 50 years ago now – and the apprenticeship took me at least 6 years.

To ensure quality, I make one item a day at the most. According to the traditional method, the wooden slabs are to be joined with bamboo pegs, but the present practice in most cases is to glue the slabs together – for the sake of convenience. I usually use Chinese fir, a soft timber, while some other kinds of timber are too hard to be worked on with tools. Timber with fewer gnarls is preferred, because items made from such timber are good-looking and resistant to water leakage. All the timber that I buy as working material must first be sun-dried for a month, and if it gets damp halfway through the work, I have to bring it out on a fine day for thorough sun-drying. Why is my place a workshop? I sell what I make – that's called a workshop.

In the past, there were a lot of practical uses for wooden buckets: rice was kept in wooden buckets, and a wok had a wooden lid – all these are circular wooden objects. Now, some people still come to buy wooden foot-washing basins, and they like the basins to have a high rim for winter, and a low rim for summer. A piece of advice before washing your feet in such a basin: put some cold water in the new basin and let it be; the wood will expand a little after absorbing water, so the basin gets even tighter and won't leak at all.

¥255 藤椅
rattan chair

藤 rattan, 78 × 56 × 58cm

¥260 铁锅
iron wok

金属 metal
9 × Ø35cm

铁锅制作过程 The manufacturing process of an iron wok

做这行需要技术，也需要力气

口述：陶师傅，54岁，熟铁匠，虹口区舟山路

我接触这个行当已经30年了，我喜欢挤在像我爸爸这样年纪的人里面交流，所以在上海，我们这辈人里我的手艺可以说算是比较精的了。

这个锅子很早以前在民间就有了，它传热快，不黏底，不变形，里面不带一点化学成分，全靠手工来做的。工序很简单，形状事先放样，画好线，剪好，然后开始敲呀。做这行需要技术，也需要力气。人家一般都不肯露自己手艺的，我么是因为要让大家知道这个真的是我手工敲的，才摆出来，不出来人家不相信的呀。

这些工具、模具很多都是自己做的，这个里面牵涉到很多工种，不是说你学一样东西，就可以做了，是汇拢了各种技术。

我一天做一两个东西，现在也不会拼命地做，要考虑到身体了。顾客要的都是比较实用的，饭勺、汤勺、铜脸盆、铜饭碗，有很多外国人和华人厨师，经常来我这边买的。可能我今后也还会有些设计作品，这个是要等到空下来，心情好要，不能急，慢慢做，细巧的东西做起来时间很长的。

Narrator: Mr. Tao, 54, wrought ironsmith, Zhoushan Road, Hongkou District

I have been in this trade for over 30 years. I like to mingle with the people of my father's age, because it is hard to find an ironsmith as skillful as me in my own generation.

This wok? It is a popular model that's been used for a long time. It is easily heated, non-sticky, non-deformable, and contains no harmful chemicals. I make these woks completely by hand. The working procedure is actually quite simple: prepare the design, draw out the lines, cut out a sheet of iron, and hammer away! This trade requires both skills and strength. Most of my fellow ironsmiths are unwilling to demonstrate their skills; I put this wok on display because I want to show people the sound proof of my handiwork.

As for these tools and molds, I made most of them myself. This profession actually involves a variety of disciplines, so don't expect to be able to make an item by simply learning to make it for there are a lot of skills at work.

I make one or two items a day. I don't work too hard now, due to health concerns. My customers come to me for practical items, such as rice ladles, soup ladles, brass basins, brass rice bowls, etc. Cooks and expatriates are especially fond of my wares. I'm planning to create some "designer" stuff in the future, though that'll have to wait until I have enough free time and a good mood. No push, just relaxed work – it takes a good while to make elegant things.

店铺、博物馆
Shops & Museums

⌂ 地址 Address
🕐 营业时间 Opening
¥ 收费 Ticket
⚲ 轨道交通 Metro
🚌 公交车 Bus

⌂ 朱家角竹器店
青浦区朱家角镇泗泾街32号
🕐 7:00-19:00
🚌 普安路汽车站→沪朱高速快线→朱家角镇

⌂ Zhujiajiao Bamboo Shop
32 Sijing Street, Zhujiajiao Town, Qingpu District
🕐 7:00-19:00
🚌 Pu'an Road Bus Station→ Huzhu Expressway Line →Zhujiajiao Town

⌂ 新场白铁铺
浦东新区新场镇新场老街207号
🕐 7:00-18:00
🚇 2、7号线→龙阳路站→🚌 龙平芦专线至新场镇

⌂ Xinchang Tinker Shop
207 Xinchang Old Street, Xinchang Town, Pudong New Area
🕐 7:00-18:00
🚇 Line 2、7 → Longyang Road Station → 🚌 Line Longpinglu → Xinchang Town

🏠 浦东土布馆
浦东新区新场镇洪西街49号
🕐 10:00-18:00
🚇 2、7号线→龙阳路站→🚌龙平芦专线→
新场镇

🏠 Pudong Homespun Cloth Shop
49 Hongxi Road, Xinchang Town, Pudong New
Area
🕐 10:00-18:00
🚇 Line 2、7 → Longyang Road Station → 🚌
Line Longpinglu → Xinchang Town

🏠 州桥竹器摊
嘉定区州桥嘉定北大街
🕐 不定

🏠 Zhouqiao Bamboo Shop
Jiading North Avenue, Zhouqiao, Jiading District
🕐 Unknown

⌂ 徐行草编合作社
嘉定区徐行镇新建一路1568号文化体育服务
中心311室
🕐 8:00-17:00（周六、日休息）
🚇 11号线→嘉定北站→🚌嘉店线→新建一
路启源路站

⌂ Xuhang Straw Weavers' Commune
Room 311, Xuhang Town Cultural Center, Jiading
District
🕐 8:00-17:00 (Mon-Fri)
🚇 Line 11 → JIading N. Station →
🚌 Line Jiadian → Xinjianyi Road
Qiyuan Road Station

⌂ 杨师傅木桶店
闵行区七宝镇徐家弄11号1楼
🕐 9:00-21:00
🚇 9号线→七宝站

⌂ Yang the Cooper
1F 11 Xujialong, Qibao Town, Minhang District
🕐 9:00-21:00
🚇 Line 9 → Qibao Station

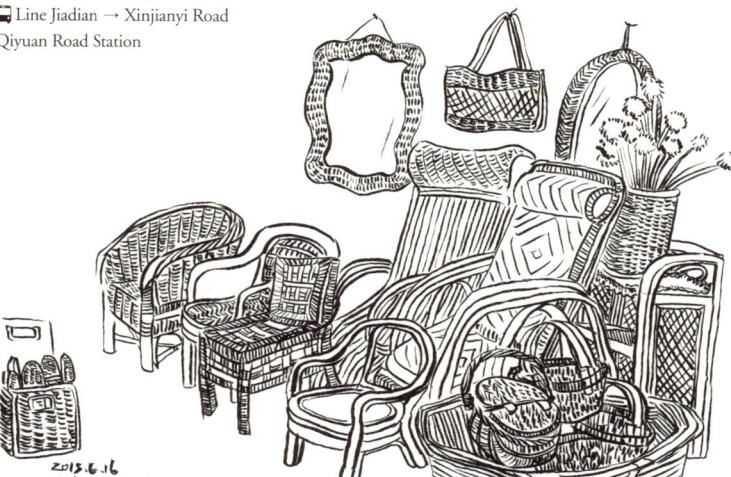

2015.6.16
瑞金二路 陈思勇画

🏠 老行当博物馆
闵行区七宝镇东街9号
🕐 9:00-17:00
¥ 5元
🚇 9号线→七宝站

🏠 Museum of Old Trades
9 East Street, Qibao Town, Minhang District
🕐 9:00-17:00
¥ 5 Yuan
🚇 Line 9 → Qibao Station

🏠 棉织坊
闵行区七宝镇北大街43号
🕐 9:00-17:00
¥ 5元
🚇 9号线→七宝站

🏠 Cotton Cloth Weaving Workshop
43 North Street, Qibao Town, Minhang District
🕐 9:00-17:00
¥ 5 Yuan
🚇 Line 9 → Qibao Station

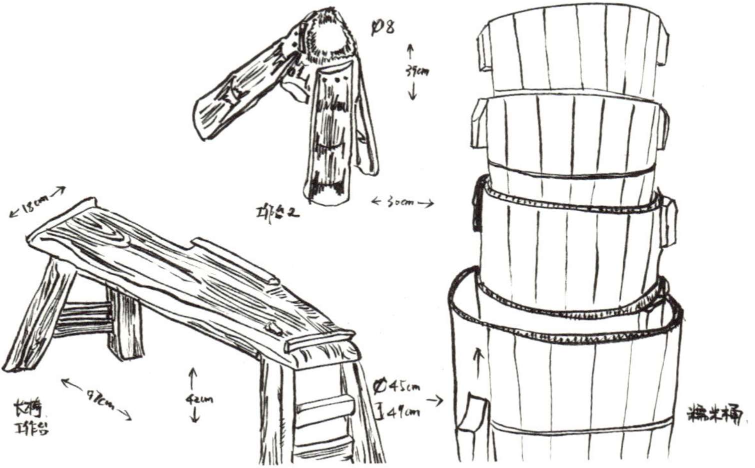

🏠 城隍庙兔子灯铺
黄浦区方浜中路373号
🕐 8:30-20:30
🚇 10号线→豫园站
注：逢农历正月初一至十五销售手工兔子
灯，平日接受预订。

🏠 Rabbit Lantern Shop of the Town God's Temple
373 Fangbang Road M., Huangpu District
🕐 8:30-20:30
🚇 Line 10 → Yuyuan Garden Station
Note: The shop offers handmade rabbit lanterns
for sale during the first half of the 1st month in the
Chinese lunar calendar and takes orders on regular
days.

🏠 顺兴泰竹器店
黄浦区中华路310号
(近复兴东路)
🕐 8:00-18:00
🚇 9号线→小东门站

🏠 Shunxingtai Bamboo Shop
310 Zhonghua Road (near Fuxing Road E.),
Huangpu District
🕐 8:00-18:00
🚇 Line 9 → Xiaodongmen Station

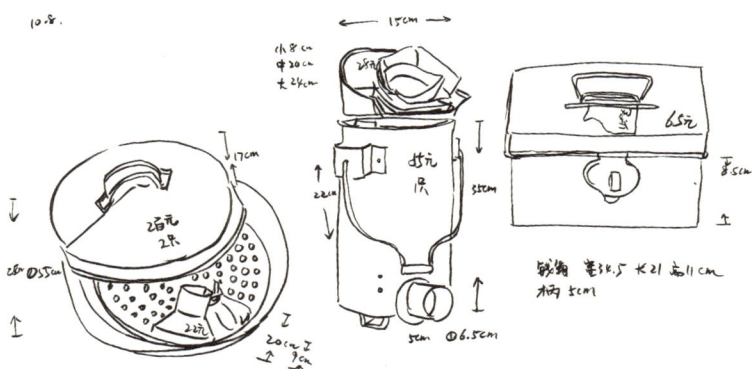

⌂ 丁娘子土布店
黄浦区方浜中路438号
🕐 10:00-17:00
🜁 10号线→豫园站

⌂ Madame Ding's Homespun Cloth Shop
438 Fangbang Road M., Huangpu District
🕐 10:00-17:00
🜁 Line 10 → Yuyuan Garden Station

⌂ 福佑路小商品市场
黄浦区福佑路沿线
🕐 6:30-17:30
🜁 10号线→豫园站

⌂ The Market of Small Objects on Fuyou Road
In the neighborhood of Fuyou Road, Huangpu
District
🕐 6:30-17:30
🜁 Line 10 → Yuyuan Garden Station

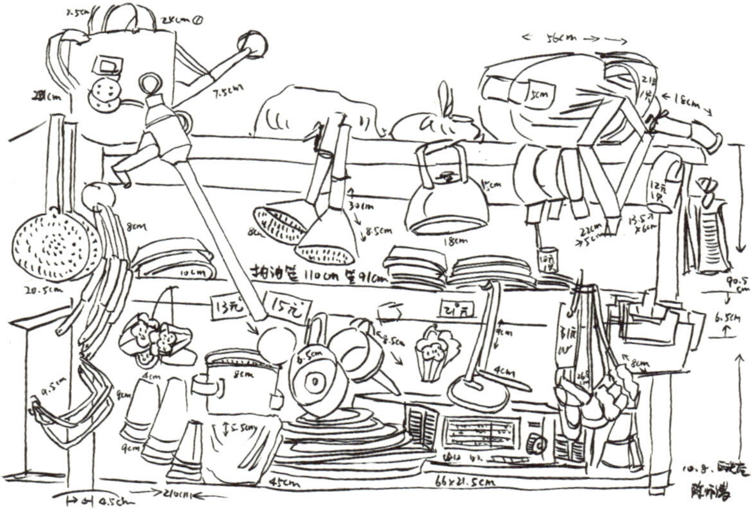

🏠 小陶手工熟铁锅
虹口区舟山路
🕐 不定

🏠 Little Tao's Handmade Wrought Iron Woks
Zhoushan Road, Hongkou District
🕐 Unknown

🏠 顺昌蒸笼店
虹口区海伦路371号 (近四平路)
🕐 8:00-19:00
🚇 4，10号线→海伦路站

🏠 Shunchang Steamer Shop
371 Hailun Road (near Siping Road), Hongkou District
🕐 8:00-19:00
🚇 Line 4，10 → Hailun Road Station

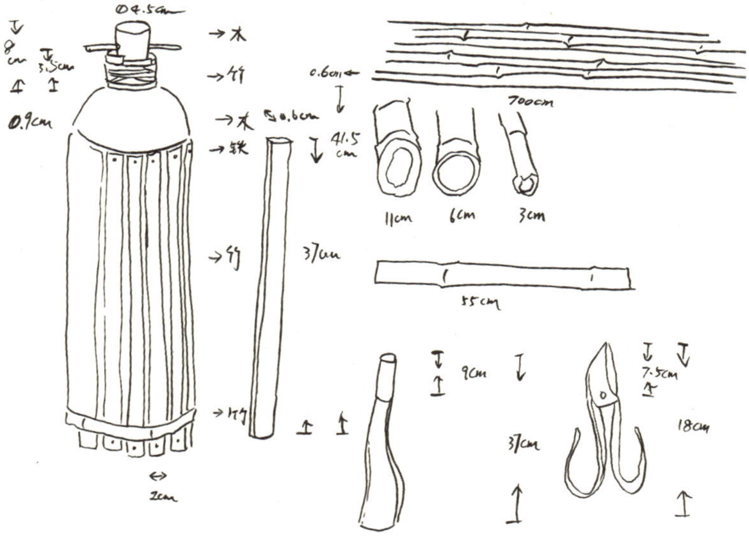

🏠 北京百货商店
静安区石门二路156号 (近北京西路)
🕐 9:00-17:00
🚇 2号线→南京西路站

🏠 Beijing Department Store
156 Shimen Road No.2 (near Beijing Road W.),
Jing'an District
🕐 9:00-17:00
🚇 Line 2 → Nanjing Road W. Station

🏠 小鸡啄米
静安区南京西路1025弄静安别墅81号1楼
🕐 12:00-20:00 (周一休息)
🚇 地铁2号线→南京西路站

🏠 Chickens Peck at Rice
1F 81 Jing'an Villas, 1025 Nanjing Road W.,
Jing'an District
🕐 12:00-20:00 (Tue-Sun)
🚇 Line 2 → Nanjing Road W. Station

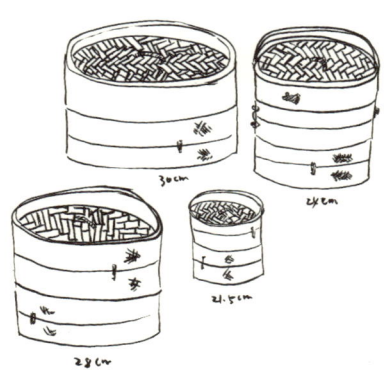

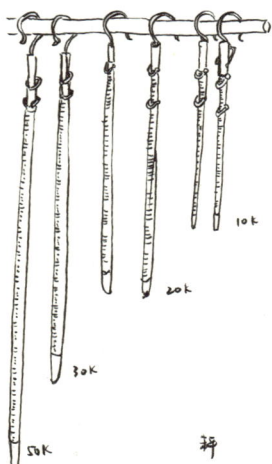

🏠 田园藤业
黄浦区瑞金二路77号（近皋兰路）
🕐 9:30-20:00
🚇 1, 10号线→陕西南路站

🏠 Tianyuan Rattan Co.
77 Ruijin Road No.2 (near Gaolan Road), Huangpu District
🕐 9:30-20:00
🚇 Line 1, 10 → Shaanxi Road S. Station

🏠 上海南方日用品有限公司
徐汇区襄阳南路223号
🕐 9:00-17:00
🚇 1, 10号线→陕西南路站

🏠 Shanghai South Daily Necessities Co., Ltd.
223 Xiangyang Road S., Xuhui District
🕐 9:00-17:00
🚇 Line 1, 10 → Shaanxi Road S. Station

🏠 城市山民
徐汇区复兴西路133号
🚌 96路 → 复兴西路武康路
黄浦区泰康路248弄14号
🚇 9号线 → 打浦桥站
🕐 10:00-22:00

🏠 Urban Tribe
133 Fuxing Road W., Xuhui District
🚌 Line 96 → Fuxing Road W. Wukang Road
248/14 Taikang Road, Huangpu District
🚇 Line 9 → Dapuqiao Station
🕐 10:00-22:00

www.urbantribe.cn

🏠 中国蓝印花布馆
徐汇区长乐路637弄24号
🕐 9:00-17:00
🚇 1，7号线 → 常熟路站

🏠 Chinese HandPrinted BlueNankeen Exhibition Hall
637/24 Changle Road, Xuhui District
🕐 9:00-17:00
🚇 Line 1, 7 → Changshu Road Station

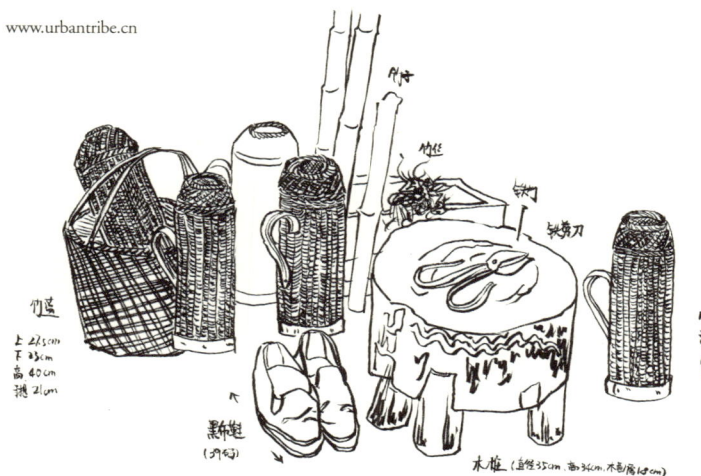

🏠 昊诚商行
徐汇区太原路126号
🕐 9:30-17:00
🚌 42路→太原路永嘉路

🏠 搭界
黄浦区泰康路248弄5号
🕐 10:00-21:00
🚇 9号线→打浦桥站

🏠 Haocheng Firm
126 Taiyuan Road, Xuhui District
🕐 9:30-17:00
🚌 Line 42 → Taiyuan Road Yongjia Road

🏠 Link Shanghai
248/5 Taikang Road, Huangpu District
🕐 10:00-21:00
🚇 Line 9 → Dapuqiao Station

⌂ 黄道婆纪念馆
徐汇区徐梅路700号
🕐 8:30-16:00

⌂ Huang Daopo Memorial House
700 Xumei Road, Xuhui District
🕐 8:30-16:00

⌂ 马路流动杂货摊
不定
🕐 不定

⌂ Traveling Peddlers
Unknown
🕐 Unknown

《留住手艺》，（日）盐野米松，广西师范大学出版社，2012

《ニッポンの老铺デザイン》，Casa BRUTUS，2011

《寻百工》，祁台颖，林品仪，纪岱昀，廖禄祯，远流出版事业股份有限公司，2010

《京都いっぴん日用品》，古濑ヒロ，淡交社，2010

Obsessive Consumption, Kate Bingaman-Burt, Princeton Architectural Press, 2010

Phaidon Design Classics, Editors of Phaidon Press, Phaidon Press, 2006

《中国制造》*China Products*，（日）岛尾伸三、潮田登久子，PAROL，2005

《天工开物》，（明）宋应星，国际文化出版社，1995

《中国手工业概论》，高叔康，商务印书馆，1947

《上海棉布》，徐蔚南，中华书局，1937

Chinese Baskets, Berthold Laufer, Field Museum of Natural History, 1925

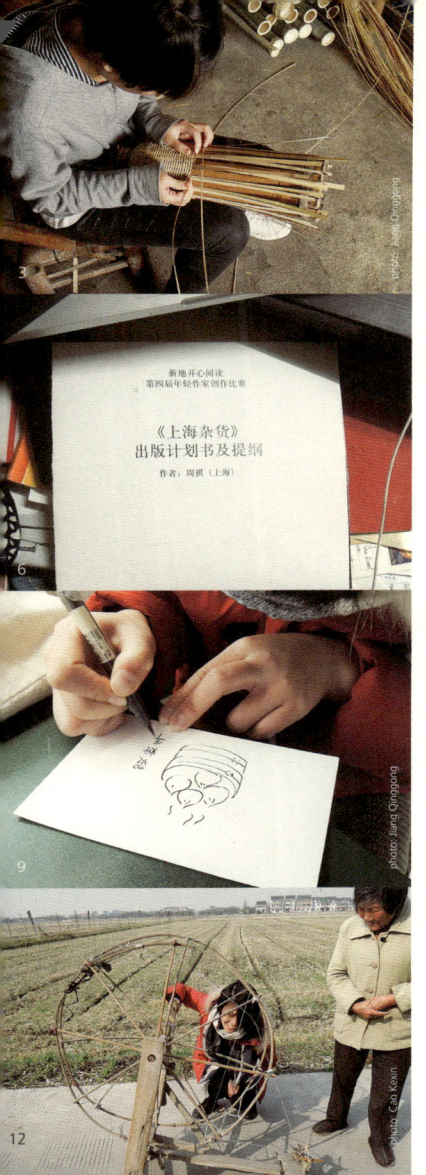

创作过程
The Making of the Book

2012年4-12月：
1 阅读的部分书籍
2 创作笔记
3 在朱家角镇采访、体验
4 在朱家角镇写生
5 参加"朱家角百多图"之绘画作品《朱家角多手艺人》

2013年1-2月：
6 参加香港"新地开心阅读——第四届年轻作家创作比赛"
7 日本京都的杂货店
8 参观日本东京下町风俗资料馆
9 手绘贺年明信片
10 新场镇路边的人造花摊
11, 12 在亭林镇采访手工织布
13 拍摄杂货素材

2013年2-7月：
14 采访顺昌竹器店
15 采访徐行镇草编手作人
16 在平安镇采访手工织布
17 老城厢街头的鞋摊
18 购买的杂货
19 在《新民晚报》上刊载"上海杂货铺"专栏
20 在平安镇采访手工织布
21 为读者准备礼物——竹蜻蜓
22 修改稿件
23 创作中使用的工具
24 作者周祺

12

photos: Jiang Qingqing

April – December 2012:

1 Looking through books of reference

2 Making notes

3 Doing interviews in a visit in Zhujiajiao

4 Drawing a sketch in Zhujiajiao

5 *Plenty of Craftsmen in Zhujiajiao*, a drawing for the "Plenty in Zhujiajiao" contest

January – February 2013:

6 Taking part in the SHKP Book Club – the Fourth Young Writers' Debut Competition

7 A grocery store in Kyoto, Japan

8 Visiting a folk art museum in Tokyo, Japan

9 A handmade New Year card

10 A roadside stall of artificial flowers in Xinchang Town

11, 12 Interviewing local workers about homespun cloth in Tinglin Town

13 Photographing the miscellaneous items

February – July 2013:

14 Doing an interview in Shunchang Bamboo Shop

15 Interviewing a straw weaver in Xuhang Town

16 Interviewing local workers about homespun cloth in Ping'an Town

17 A shoemaker's stall in the Shanghai Old Town

18 A large purchase of various items

19 A column of "Shanghai Housewares" on Shanghai's evening newspaper *Xinmin Wanbao*

20 Interviewing local workers about homespun cloth in Ping'an Town

21 Preparing the gifts for readers – bamboo copters

22 Making amendments to the draft

23 The equipment for making the book

24 Zhou Qi, the author of the book

图书在版编目（CIP）数据

上海杂货铺／周祺著. -- 上海: 同济大学出版社,
2013.8

ISBN 978-7-5608-5240-9

Ⅰ.①上…Ⅱ.①周…Ⅲ.①日用品－介绍－上海市
Ⅳ.①TS976.8

中国版本图书馆CIP数据核字 (2013) 第183358号

上海杂货铺

周祺　著

出品 人：支文军
责任编辑：张　翠
责任校对：徐春莲
出版发行：同济大学出版社 www.tongjipress.com.cn
地　　址：上海市四平路1239号　邮编：200092
电　　话：021－65985622
经　　销：全国新华书店
印　　刷：上海雅昌彩色印刷有限公司
开　　本：787mm×1 092mm　1/36
印　　张：4
印　　数：1－4 100
字　　数：100 000
版　　次：2013年8月第1版　2013年8月第1次印刷
书　　号：ISBN 978－7－5608－5240－9
定　　价：48.00元